CHET PICKENS

CLP PRODUCTIONS Art Studio Inc.
978-1-7354962-3-8
All rights reserved
Copyright © 2020

INTRODUCTION

　　Growing up in the 70's was a very exciting time for me. It was a time when everyone seemed to know each other in the community. I grew up on the south eastside of my city. The community consisted of three high-rise buildings that faced one another. The buildings were located at a dead end area; they were sixteen stories high and there was a very large round open area in the middle of them. This area was all concrete with a sidewalk around it. We called it the "skating ring". This is where most of the action took place. People would meet from the different buildings to play all sorts of games like softball, tag, skating, or just to walk around it. I attended a trailer park school; it was a group of trailers for different grade levels. After school we often got into mischief, we climbed old buildings, threw rocks, and walked the railroad tracks that ran near by. The set of tracks we walked was no longer in service, it went so far then cut off, it was supported on a large concrete bridge where grass had grown over most of it and located next to that were the metro tracks that we dared not to go near. A few blocks down in an isolated area next to a group of buildings, was a narrow opening, it was the entrance to a long steel bridge that was used to cross over the railroad tracks and the eight lanes of expressway, before reaching the beautiful lakefront area where we played from time to time.

　　Most of the games we played were pretending to be the characters from the TV shows we watched like the Japanese sci-fi adventures, the series were very popular and everyone picked their favorite character from their show. Most of our energy went into arguing about hypothetical situations, "my guy beat your guy because his power is greater" or the other person's character didn't have the ability to do the imaginary super power that person had pretended to do. We would go on and on till we finally got tired or something else got our attention.

　　I often sat on the couch for hours at a time looking out the window at the pigeons. I loved birds but tropical fish was my favorite. I noticed everything, sometimes to the smallest detail. I remember being so excited the first time I visited the local airport I seen large airplanes and trucks up close. I was so intrigued; when I got home I sketched them. From then on what ever excited me I sketched it, Soon I began to sketch little figures that represented the friends in my class, those little people later developed into comics. Everyone would always say how sweet the characters looked. I began calling them the Candy Gang. The Candy Gang is a comic strip that consists of various characters with a 70's theme. The story starts out around the lakefront high-rise apartment buildings. These children don't have the traditional play toys other children have, making their community their playground. They often get into mischief but along the way they never fail to lend a helping hand. They are truly sweet, and it's possible we'll see ourselves in some part of their story. Growing up, I watched a lot of cartoons and read the comic section of the newspaper when my dad was finished. My very first attempts were comic scenes, then comic stories. It often took many days and hours to finish a project. Many of them were never completed due to a lack of experience at the time. I would either lose interest or run out of ideas. I created the Candy Gang when I was ten years old, the characters represent the children that I grew up with and I named most of the characters after them.

Character Chet is a dreamer, his dreams give me a chance to let my imagination run wild, he can become anything, there are endless possibilities, this is what makes the strip different from most other strips. The dreams can be from the past or far in the future but when Chet dreams, he usually dreams of becoming "Superfly" the hero, the series will certainly keep us on the edge with the high-powered fast paced mystery of the never-ending saga. His powers include a (cool brim) hat he wears. It can be used to deflect evil death rays or as a Frisbee to cut down his enemies, his 'mega spin', knocks his foes to the ground, then he pounces, runs and uses his athletic abilities to defeat his foes, there's action from panels to panel and page to page. Many artists have inspired me with their ability to share their story thru their work. Growing up I enjoyed reading daily strips from the comic section of the newspaper. At age thirteen I won my first major drawing contest and was awarded a golden key Scholastic art award from my state. The Candy Gang has been apart of my art creations from a very early age, I sketched the backgrounds for my own projects; my work was dated and kept in a safe place. Many of my comic ideas come from things I enjoy.

CANDY GA

THIS LITTLE GROUP OF CHARACTERS IS SURE TO STEAL YOUR HEART. THEY'RE CUTE, LOVEABLE AND ALWAYS ON THE GO, SO HANG ON TIGHT CAUSE YOU'RE IN FOR THE RIDE OF YOUR LIFE. THESE CHARACTERS IS SO ADORABLE AND UNIQUE READERS WILL FALL IN LOVE WITH THEM!

A MESSAGE FROM CLP PRODUCTIONS

INTRODUCING... CANDY GANG™

JUST WHEN YOU THINK THEY'RE DONE THEY BOUNCE BACK IN FULL FORCE SO COME AND JOIN IN ON THE LAUGHS.

CANDY GANG  **CHET PICKENS**

CANDY GANG  **CHET PICKENS**

CANDY GANG **CHET PICKENS**

CANDY GANG **CHET PICKENS**

CANDY GANG — **OLD SKOOL COMICS** — **CHET PICKENS**

FOUR SQUARE

CANDY GANG — **CHET PICKENS**

CANDY GANG — **CHET PICKENS**

OLD SKOOL COMICS

CANDY GANG
original drawing 5/1/92

Original story boards like this one has been re-drawn

CANDY GANG

original drawing 12-15-81

original drawing 2-12-82

original drawing 12-3-82

I've always wanted to be a cartoonist and hoped that someday my comics would be in the newspaper too. Above is some strips I pretended to prepare for the newspaper.

I still have most of my child-hood drawings and original drawing tablet I've always dated my projects. Above is the date I started working on my book "Mischief Makers" and a drawing of some characters I used for a comic story. The characters was inspired from the comic strip "Tumbleweeds" by Tom Ryan. My sketch pads is also my comic diary.

I've always enjoyed watching animal shows and reading about them in books. I drew the animals I liked the most like, fish, badgers and wolves. Soon after I began creating short stories with my characters. Many of the original child-hood drawings and ideas are still used.

As I've grown so have the characters. I've always created the characters and art work for all to enjoy. Below is an old favorite drawing that I made into a poster.

"2006" POSTER OF AN OLD DRAWING

ORIGINAL DRAWING 2/19/82

COMIC STORY PENCIL DRAWING "79"

It often took many hours and days to finish a project like this. Many of them were never completed due to a lack of experience at the time. I would either lose interest or run out of ideas. I've always loved animals. I watched many educational programs about them but I usually didn't use an all-animal cast to tell my comic story, making this one very rare.

ceramic figure of "DOOLITTLE"

COMIC STORY PENCIL DRAWING "79"

Many cartoonist have inspired me with their work. This is a comic story I created using the likeness of the Tumbleweeds characters that was created by Tim Ryan.

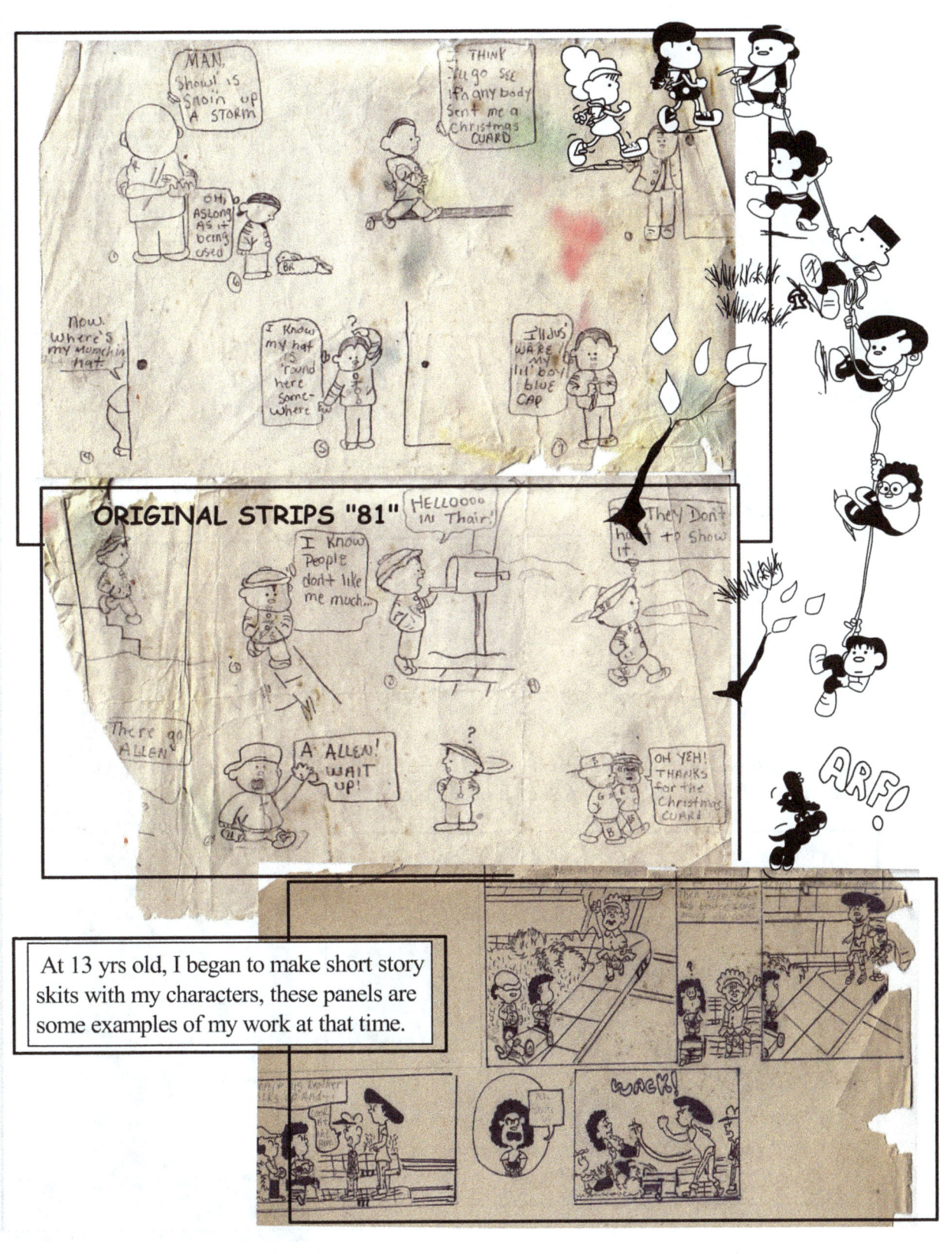

ORIGINAL STRIPS "81"

At 13 yrs old, I began to make short story skits with my characters, these panels are some examples of my work at that time.

I often sketched areas around my neighborhood for the background scenes of my comic strips. An 80's sketch of our home in the suburbs with some wishful thinking by Doolittle.

Football, baseball and basketball has always been fun to play and bringing the fun to the strip is always a challenge.(Above) A sketch of the boys playing baseball

I've always dreamed of being a cartoonist. This year I finally got that chance with the 'Insight Newspaper' located in the St. Paul, Minnesota area, thanks to editors Batala McFarlane and Adrianne Butler.

Along the way I've had many supporters, starting here at Triton College with Kathy Navilio giving me my first publication in the Fifth Ave Journal and Carol Clover of the Maywood library, in my hometown. I've been invited to show my work not only at the black history expo but the library allowed me to showcase the Candy Gang strips and posters all year in their own section of the library on the first floor.

Being a student here at Triton College has giving me the necessary skills to advertise and design.

Chet

CANDY GANG

A, B, C, D, E, F, G

H, I, J, K, ..

HMMM?

ELLA, MINO, P...

CHET PICKENS

NOW I KNOW MY A,B,C'S NEXT TIME WANT YOU SAY WITH ME....

CANDY GANG CREATED AND WRITTEN BY CHET PICKENS COPYRIGHT©2008 pickenschet@hotmail.com
ALL RIGHTS RESERVED. CANDY GANG CHARACTERS ©COPYRIGHT 2005

fifthave@triton.edu

This is one of several articles, about the Candy Gang, that has been published by the 5th Avenue Journal newspaper.

DO-TOO CERAMIC FIGURE
CLP PRODUCTIONS Copyright© 2008

IKE CERAMIC FIGURE
CLP PRODUCTIONS Copyright© 2008

ORIGINAL DRAWING 2/19/82

I'd spend days trying to create a strip but many of my childhood strips would go unfinished

Many ideas come to mind and they are quickly sketched. The strip has many chilld-hood songs and musical lyrics. Education is also a part of the strip along with other useful fun facts.

CLASSIC COLLECTION

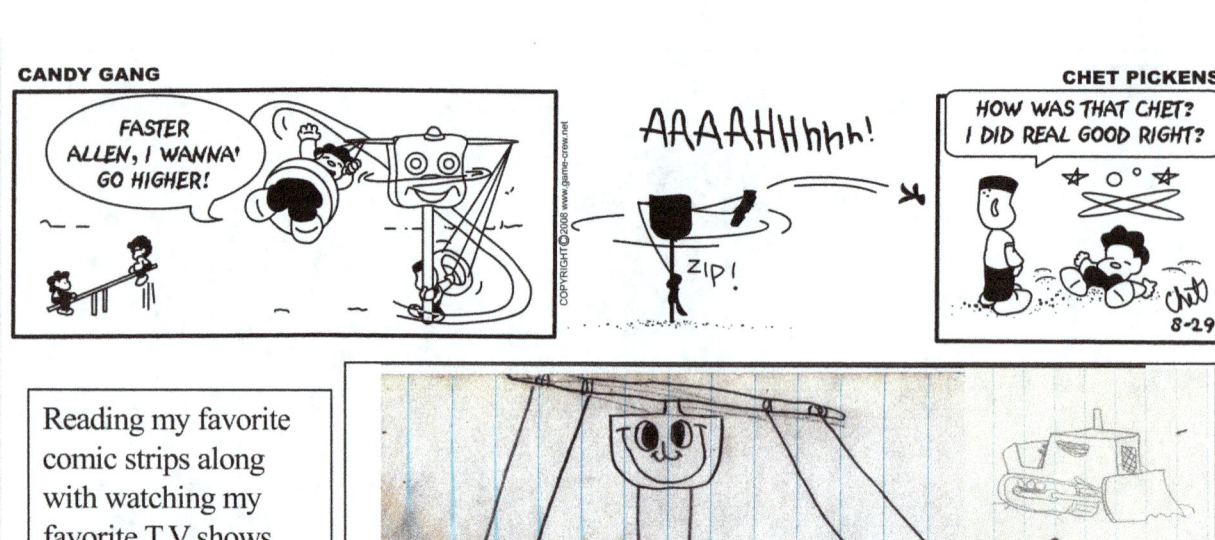

Reading my favorite comic strips along with watching my favorite T.V shows inspired many of my drawings.
My child-hood sketches of our playground was used to create the strip above.

CANDY GANG

COLOR MARKER DRAWING "78"

Coming up with the four panel strips is fun but the one panels are just as much fun too, it has given me a chance to express myself and get straight to the point. What started as a doodle job for a possible art project became serious works.

The Candy Gang celebrated Black History month with these educational panels. Movies and sports has alway been interesting. These panels celebrate African American actor James Earl Jones and boxing Champion Jack Johnson.

Ike is the neighborhood dog, he's often misunderstood by his adopted owner Chet. He thinks Ike is a tough dog and is constantly testing him but he's not. Ike joined the gang much later replacing the original dog named "Ace".

Afro combs, soul picks, peace signs, love and happiness were all signs of the times. Dance shows were a big hit too, it gave everyone a chance to show some soul. If you wore some bell bottom pants with some cool stack shoes you were definately hip. Besides the sporty everyday gear the gang wears, they definately dress hip in their 70's attire.

Marilyn is the girl all the boys seem to like and Chet is no exception. Just when it seems he has her where he wants her, everything is not what it seems.

CANDY GANG

CHET IS A DREAMER, IN HIS DREAMS THERE ARE ENDLESS ADVENTURES IN THE STRIP. THE DREAMS CAN BE FAR IN THE PAST OR FUTURE BUT WHEN CHET DREAMS HE USUALLY DREAMS OF BECOMING SUPER FLY THE HERO. THE SERIES WILL CERTAINLY KEEP US ON EDGE WITH THE HIGH POWERED, FAST PACED MYSTERY OF THE NEVER ENDING - SAGA.

The art of the Candy Gang have included, simple game creations, that can be played for free and found on various websites. All the games include one or more of the characters. It has also included the art of ceramics. Hand-crafting the Candy Gang characters was a challenge for me because it was my first attempt.

SUPERFLY ADVENTURES

The 2007 Black History Expo at the Maywood public library was a great experience, where I met many interesting people. It was the first public introduction of the Candy Gang characters.

www.ingramcontent.com/pod-product-compliance
Lightning Source LLC
Chambersburg PA
CBHW081128080526
44587CB00021B/3793